JOHN DANCED

JOHN DANCED

Gail Rudd

BERKELEY POETS' WORKSHOP & PRESS 1982

ISBN 0-917658-20-5

Acknowledgement is made to the following publications
where some of these poems have appeared:

> *Denver Quarterly, Handbook, Kansas*
> *Quarterly, Ohio Journal, Pontchartrain*
> *Review, Ragazine.*

Cover photograph by Craig Schmitt.

Typesetting: Ampersand Typography; Berkeley, California
Printing: Braun-Brumfield, Inc.; Ann Arbor, Michigan

For John Randolph Rudd: 1907-1973

CONTENTS

3   What Annie Wants

8   Giving

9   December 4

10   Waking Death Dream

12   Daddy I

13   30

14   The Dream

15   The Only One

16   Ross

18   Daddy II

19   Two Letters

22   The Dance

23   Daddy III

24   Living

WHAT ANNIE WANTS

1

Ann turns toward the light
moving in the garden below
Her hair is flowing
The night air is palpable gardenia
Her nightgown blows between her legs
as she stands at the window
breathing

But she goes down
She puts on her big work shoes
and takes the silver high beam
flashlight from the drawer
and goes down
striding with purpose
into the gardenias

Swallowing fear
her light swallows up the smaller light
in the garden

2

She is wanting to touch him
her bones are leaning
into his
She is feeling the insides of him
with her mind
She is swimming naked in the pool
in the cave of his body
lit only by his eyes
far above
looking in at her

But she gets out
Every time she gets out
and touches his coat sleeve
Cautiously she explains it:
Kinship kindred kindle
Her looking pushes him back
into his chair
behind his desk

She touches his forehead
checking for fever
suggests dry heat

3

Small Annie is sitting on a lawn chair
in the pouring rain
her umbrella orange
on grey and green
There are bunnies in the cabbage
strange long-legged birds
beside the pine tree
Annie is disappearing
into the sound of rain
every follicle straining
into the droplets
following her mind

Ann gets up
She stands in the parking lot
beside the pier in the pouring rain
and swivels in her shoes
She goes back
She turns her longing over
and puts it into the drawer
of her metal desk
She sits down,
the window
at her back.

4

Ann looks over bones
to her face
shining in candlelight
and sees
irises

Annie knows roses
unashamed
in their quick full blooms
What is this spareness
this shy spring flower
lacking conviction?

5

Annie hungers for maps
and the man with glasses
but she needs
the man
who is there
in the morning.

GIVING

For me, it is drambuie:
molten in the mouth,
carefully held, and swallowed
in time, savoring the
burning thickness slipping
into me, and holding the
black bright shine
for long quiet breaths
in the dark
of your oblivious
grateful death.

Below you, my
tear-cornered eyes
grow used again
to the dark

and i let go
blowing the light
back into you
letting you go.

For you, it is done:
we are loved
we are mingled
we sleep.

DECEMBER 4

This is the sixth year that we have been without you
and we are still living.
When our smooth surfaces begin to bubble
under the heat from your remembered light
we get busy
we write down our dreams
we stare out of bus windows
into rush hours and sunset
and in the smallest moments of black time
our surfaces erupt.

In the mornings' soot we are pock-marked
with tiny finished volcanos.
Someone is bringing paint
But you are still dead
and we are dying.

WAKING DEATH DREAM

Slipping, i fall down between
the slices of night
into my coffin
my skin is layering off
in places, brittle as onion skin
the horror bursts in upon me
swelling my stomach with fear
nauseated, my hands and feet
go numb
                i remember
creamy circles of my cheeks
in the mirror and the acid
fantasy of my bones bared and glaring;
this is real. I am bone
or, like my father, burned
and ash
                this comes to me
out of the black in a scream
of pain; what if he felt
the flames? . . .
                        and you, beside me,
heavy now with sleep—(i slide
my arm over you, lay my palm
against your heart, fold my knees into
the hollows of yours) you
suddenly cold and damp
and i not knowing
whether you are there
your warm flesh not
answering mine; here, at your hip,
this flat white bone
and under my hand: nothing
will beat or seek . . .
                        i must go back.

Surely the spirit flies
Surely it's as i've said before:
the body spoiled meat
Dispose of it quickly in whatever way
Shed and forget the rotted chrysalis
in the first sure light . . .
                            the skylight
pulls me up—the pale square
opening to something
Is it the first or the last light?

DADDY I

We are dancing, Daddy
Benny Goodman's molten notes
sliding through the air
Bing Crosby crooning
as my silver slippers stutter
over the carpet in my passion
simple and pure
for your arms.

Daddy, we are gliding
over the floor,
behind my eyes, the ballroom
at Euclid Beach, glittering
chandeliers, candelabra, tear-drops,
wrist corsages; i am my mother
we are the center of the evening.

Oh Daddy, this time it is more
We have gone one step beyond
the loosing of bras
for the ritual scratching
of my back, into the kissing
into the real touching
and it is almost
too much
Daddy, dance with me
dance with me
again.

30

Waking slowly, thick from the yellow world
into light
i am paralyzed in hot sleep
and the feeling comes back
last, to my hands.

Half-curled,
lobster-claws, they move
across the sheet
painfully
flexing into consciousness
against the fibers
binding them to sleep
coiling and recoiling
from day.

First microscopic seed
of death
silently entering my fingertips
at thirty
growing slowly: an aching
salt clotting in my joints.

Lifting the breakfast plates
the numbness spreads through my palm
the first tendril of pain
licks in my wrist
and what i say, smiling,
is not what i feel.

Before we sleep
i am warm and animated
flexible and flowing—
i sigh and smile
murmuring "tomorrow"
and on my pillow, by my cheek,
my fingers begin to curl.

THE DREAM

Into my father's dream
i wind, night and again
i sit among the young folks
in the hay wagon, laughing
and singing, my father young
and ruddy amongst us
singing sweet tenor into the night trees
laden with heavy sleeping birds.

We pass, under the moon,
my father, old, standing in the road,
his earnest blue eyes washed
with remembering; he's been working . . .
coming home tired. He lifts
his hand into the night
and smiles; we pass into dark.

In the small moments of peace
i wind back through the dark
seeking that place in the path
where my father stands
watching the dream.

THE ONLY ONE

I unbraided my hair
It brushed out in auburn waves
and i went downstairs.

My father's face flashed
recognition
and he said, "It's so beautiful,
your hair.
Come sit by me;
you are the unselfish one,
the only one
like me."

Later, after lovers,
"Take care.
You are the unselfish one "
And i wouldn't go to him
his visions having come to lies.

After he died
i cut my hair.
I kept it close to my head
and tight.

I fear he knew
at last
what all his hopes
had come to—

He was the only one.

ROSS

Moby Dick spouting silver fountains in the dark,
baby whales inside the great protective circle,
the waters aspen-gold with brit,
that whale food, and Ahab planted on the forecastle
like a lightning-severed tree
i see, i see you kneeling
carving poems in your wide flat forearm
and your blood
drops in berries piling in my lap.

At dawn in mescaline
you come with violets almost smothering
a red rose (she breaks free)
You send orchids from Taiwan
and Okinawa
and always, rima, rima
from the forecastle watch.

I have a photograph
your brown beard looking grey
your chest rising and falling beneath
the dog-tags
silver as the moon above your ship.

You fell, buddy,
you fell from me
after you caught the garter . . .
and you went in sopors, in cocaine, in dreams.

In dreams you said last night,
right in the middle of Moby Dick,
"Do you want to buy a vacuum cleaner?"
and i reached for you
trying to touch you this time
You backed up wildly
shouting "No"
and i knew i had gone too far
I kept saying that i wanted you
but i wondered who you were
and buddy
who the hell you thought i was.

DADDY II

You are hurrying
through the blue light, Daddy
you are pink and powdered
and smelling like my own legs

my salt-tasting knees
dim far hush of cars
below my window
charmed with fastening your garters
over your smooth calves
in the mornings
before we go for the cleaning
for liquor, milk, and lemon cokes
(you grab my shoulder once
saying i must respond to your voice
immediately
without question)

i love your neck
and long before other arms
in other furry coats
so far in their blackness
from your red-gold sheath
are loving me

oh, Daddy, you were loving me
as i fill my lungs
with salt water taffy
and approach the final hill
of the roller coaster
screaming over the side
you are smiling
you know
it is the right time
for screaming.

TWO LETTERS

I see it sometimes
as a fine line drawing
on onionskin,
bright thread lines of color,
teepees, swing sets, legs
and other open triangles.

Very tired in the afternoons
i moved slowly
feeling the exact weight
of every gesture
knowing the texture
of my own flesh
viewing the world through gauze
like first spring
tentative
carefully eating
bread and milk in a bowl,
peaches, ice cream—
folding soft things
around my body lovingly.

The night before it ended
it rained.
I lay, accepting those praises,
the soft swelling of a plum
growing under my hand
in the dark
my fingers tracing
the gentle curve of breasts
too tender, too full
for touch.

She would have been like you:
spare, angular, remote
with great animal eyes
knowing what they know—
saying things to make me
blink and laugh
and sit a long time
in silence
thirty years of waiting
snowing over her infancy.

Oh, it would have been mad
They might have locked me,
broken, torn and crazy,
for such powerful rage
if the dream fell false
into the world.

She would have been like you:
not full and urgent,
pear-shaped, florid,
thick with thinking and fear,
but lean, geometric and detached,
light with the absence of futility,
other pictures
behind her eyes.

I would have touched her,
a female person,
in the righteous intimacy
of ancient passion,
giving back my mother's body
into new life
with the force of all
i could have loved:
myself, my mother,
you.

Oh, I have gone and sent you off
and the cave where you were growing
shakes me with contracting spasms
in the mornings,
fighting to shut itself off
from light.

And you are looking about
at thinner, more angular women,
dreaming of tight and solid shapes
without hollow places
that swell in the night.
Your eyes are
sometimes
remote,
thinking perhaps
of someone more like you.

Sometimes I see it
as a fine line drawing
on onionskin,
bright thread lines of color
shooting out from a central shape
childishly drawn
too thick and round
a crayon sun.

THE DANCE

All night
the dance
meticulously choreographed for two
danced by four
slips flawlessly
toward morning

With fire
wolves singing outside
they weave themselves
without touching

He is wooing her
with music
his voice
a thread
leading her
into the fire
their partners dazed
and oblivious

He leads her out

The children sleep
in other rooms
dreaming fitfully of sleep
and the fire
the grown-ups make
and save you from

by this dancing.

DADDY III

Are you there?
Are you ordering milk
in a classy restaurant
full of coffee and martinis?
laying your flat palm
over the bald dome of your mind
shining and pink
in a clasp of laughter
shaking silently
before the waves break
into the room
everyone smiling with pure pleasure
at your unfeigned, unsophisticated joy?
(the same joy
over which you shamed
a poor man's pleasure
a bus driver's light
a measure of your unsuccess
under the rich Florida palms)
Are you sipping heavy wine
and inexpensive high-balls
a quick shot
rushing through your veins
your laughter
living in the dark?

LIVING

1

Too many voices have shaped my sleep
I cannot remember names
not even one.
I have tried too hard, too many times
I have bent myself so many ways
that now i cannot stand alone;
i lean.

I lean my cheek on the cool walls
of restrooms and listen
as the frightened face above the sink
explains it all again.

2

When it rains
i feel that i will wash away
sweeping small boats before me
through the gutters to the sea—
but i never go.
I diminish like granite:
a few grains to the storm.

Photo by Juliet Connolly

Gail Rudd, currently a resident of the San Francisco Bay Area, holds a Master's degree in English / Creative Writing from Ohio State University. She has taught at Ohio State, Ohio Wesleyan, and for the Creative Arts Program in Columbus, Ohio. This is the first published collection of her poems.

Also available from the Berkeley Poets' Workshop & Press;
Box 459; Berkeley, CA 94701

BERKELEY POETS COOPERATIVE ANTHOLOGY
poetry and fiction, 275 pages, $6.95
SNAKE BLOSSOMS by Belden
poetry and fiction, 64 pages, $3.00
JACKBIRD by Bruce Boston
fiction, 88 pages, $3.00
SHE COMES WHEN YOU'RE LEAVING by Bruce Boston
fiction, 64 pages, $3.95
SLOW JUGGLING by Karen Brodine
poetry, 48 pages, $3.00
SEAWARD by Betty Coon
poetry, 44 pages, $3.00
NEWSPAPER STORIES by Patricia Dienstfrey
poetry, 36 pages, $3.75
CASTING FOR THE CUTTHROAT by Charles Entrekin
poetry, 48 pages, $3.95
ALL PIECES OF A LEGACY by Charles Entrekin
poetry, 48 pages, $3.95
HALF A BOTTLE OF CATSUP by Ted Fleischman
poetry, 36 pages, $3.00
THE GHOST OF THE BUICK by Bruce Hawkins
poetry, 54 pages, $3.95
WORDROWS by Bruce Hawkins
poetry, 40 pages, $3.00
WASH ME ON HOME, MAMA by Peter Najarian
fiction, 84 pages, $3.00
ONCE MORE OUT OF DARKNESS by Alicia Ostriker
poetry, 32 pages, $3.00
OVER BY THE CAVES by Jennifer Stone
fiction, 60 pages, $3.00
THE MACHINE SHUTS DOWN by Rod Tulloss
poetry, 40 pages, $3.95
BERKELEY POETS COOPERATIVE (magazine)
poetry, fiction, graphics, 72 to 96 pages
                                Current Issue $3.00
                                Subscription   3/$10.00